Facts About the Rhinoceros

By Lisa Strattin

© 2019 Lisa Strattin

FREE BOOK

FREE FOR ALL SUBSCRIBERS

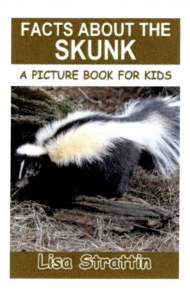

LisaStrattin.com/Subscribe-Here

BOX SET

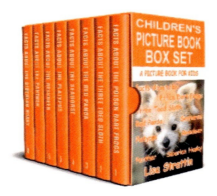

- **FACTS ABOUT THE POISON DART FROGS**
- **FACTS ABOUT THE THREE TOED SLOTH**
- **FACTS ABOUT THE RED PANDA**
- **FACTS ABOUT THE SEAHORSE**
- **FACTS ABOUT THE PLATYPUS**
- **FACTS ABOUT THE REINDEER**
- **FACTS ABOUT THE PANTHER**
- **FACTS ABOUT THE SIBERIAN HUSKY**

LisaStrattin.com/BookBundle

Facts for Kids Picture Books by Lisa Strattin

Little Blue Penguin, Vol 92

Chipmunk, Vol 5

Frilled Lizard, Vol 39

Blue and Gold Macaw, Vol 13

Poison Dart Frogs, Vol 50

Blue Tarantula, Vol 115

African Elephants, Vol 8

Amur Leopard, Vol 89

Sabre Tooth Tiger, Vol 167

Baboon, Vol 174

Sign Up for New Release Emails Here

LisaStrattin.com/subscribe-here

Contents

INTRODUCTION

The rhinoceros is a large mammal native to Africa and Asia. There are five species of rhino found in the world with 3 out of these species now considered to be critically endangered. The rhino is thought to be the second biggest land mammal in the world behind the African elephant.

The five species of rhinoceros are the White Rhino (which is the largest species of rhino) and the Black Rhino which are both native to Africa and really only differ in size as they look so much alike. The Indian Rhino, the Sumatran Rhino and the Javan Rhino are all native to Asia and are much smaller in size than the two rhino species of Africa.

CHARACTERISTICS

The rhino is prized for its horn. The horns of a rhinoceros are made of keratin, the same type of protein that makes up hair and fingernails in most animals including humans. Both African species of rhino and the Sumatran rhinoceros have two horns, while the Indian rhino and Javan rhinoceros have just one horn.

Rhinos have brilliant hearing and a keen sense of smell, but they are well known for having extremely poor eyesight.

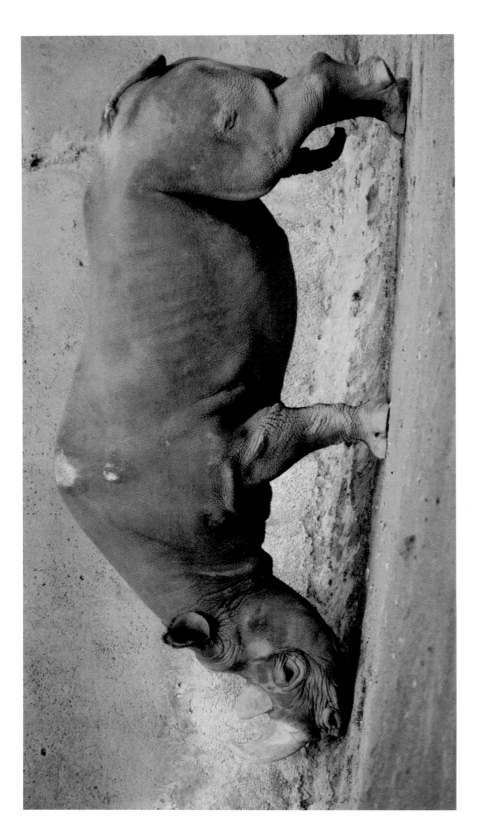

APPEARANCE

The rhinoceros is probably best known for its striking resemblance to the dinosaurs of prehistoric times. They have thick, leathery skin and the prominent horn, when you consider these features along with their size, it is not surprising that the rhino reminds us of a dinosaur!

The rhinoceros is one of the largest animals roaming our world today, second only to the elephant.

REPRODUCTION

Every two and a half to five years, a female rhino will reproduce. They carry their young for a gestation period of 15 to 16 months. They usually only have one baby at a time, though they do sometimes have twins.

LIFE SPAN

Rhinos usually live for 35 to 50 years!

SIZE

The adult rhino averages about 1.5 tons in weight and can be 4 to 7 feet long.

The various species of rhino differ in size. For example, a Black Rhino reaches an average weight of between 1,750 and 3,000 pounds, while a White Rhino can be up to three tons, or 6 000 pounds in weight. The other three species are generally smaller than these.

HABITAT

The rhinoceros is generally found in thick forests and savannas where there is plenty of food to eat and lots of cover for the rhino to hide in. Although they are herbivores, they are known for their aggressive nature and will often charge oncoming predators in order to scare them away.

DIET

The rhinoceros eats grasses, leaves, shoots, buds and fruits in order to gain the nutrients necessary to grow and survive.

ENEMIES

Adult rhinoceros have no real predators in the wild, other than people. Young rhinos are prey to big cats, crocodiles, African Wild Dogs, and hyenas.

Schristia Photography ~

SUITABILITY AS PETS

You can see rhinos in many zoos, perhaps your local zoo has a habitat where they can be watched. Of course, they are endangered, so having one as a pet is not a choice for you. Besides they are HUGE, so where would you keep one?

They are interesting to see, so if you get a chance to see them at a zoo, you should certainly visit.

COLOR ME

COLOR ME

COLOR ME

COLOR ME

COLOR ME

COLOR ME

COLOR ME

COLOR ME

Please leave me a review here:

LisaStrattin.com/Review-Vol-257

For more Kindle Downloads Visit Lisa Strattin Author Page on Amazon Author Central

amazon.com/author/lisastrattin

To see upcoming titles, visit my website at LisaStrattin.com– most books available on Kindle!

LisaStrattin.com

FREE BOOK

FOR ALL SUBSCRIBERS – SIGN UP NOW

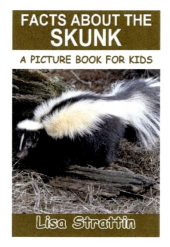

LisaStrattin.com/Subscribe-Here

LisaStrattin.com/Facebook

LisaStrattin.com/Youtube